P9-CQK-968

HOCKEY

AND ITS GREATEST PLAYERS

in side sports

HOCKEY
AND ITS GREATEST PLAYERS

EDITED BY HOPE LOURIE KILLCOYNE

Britannica®
Educational Publishing
IN ASSOCIATION WITH

ROSEN
EDUCATIONAL SERVICES

Published in 2015 by Britannica Educational Publishing (a trademark of Encyclopædia Britannica, Inc.) in association with The Rosen Publishing Group, Inc.
29 East 21st Street, New York, NY 10010

Distributed exclusively by Rosen Publishing.
To see additional Britannica Educational Publishing titles, go to rosenpublishing.com.

First Edition

Britannica Educational Publishing
J. E. Luebering: Director, Core Reference Group
Anthony L. Green: Editor, Compton's by Britannica

Rosen Publishing
Hope Lourie Killcoyne: Executive Editor
Additional content supplied by Kristen Rajczak
Nelson Sá: Art Director
Brian Garvey: Designer
Cindy Reiman: Photography Manager

Library of Congress Cataloging-in-Publication Data

Hockey and its greatest players/edited by Hope Lourie Killcoyne.—First Edition.
        pages cm.—((Inside Sports))
"Distributed exclusively by Rosen Publishing"—T.p. verso.
Includes bibliographical references and index.
ISBN 978-1-62275-586-8 (library bound)
1. Hockey—History—Juvenile literature. 2. Hockey players—Rating of. I. Killcoyne, Hope Lourie.
GV847.25.H63 2015
796.962'64—dc23

2014023132

Manufactured in the United States of America

On the cover, page 3: Jonathan Toews of the Chicago Blackhawks. *Jonathan Daniel/Getty Images*

CONTENTS

INTRODUCTION

I n 2010, Patrick Kane of the Chicago Blackhawks made a championship-winning goal that almost no one in the arena could see—including some of the players on the ice. The puck zipped past Philadelphia Flyers goalie Michael Leighton into the right corner of the net so fast and at such an angle that only a replay could confirm the Blackhawks' win. The speed and abruptness of Kane's goal highlights the changeable, exciting nature of ice hockey. It is the fastest of all team sports.

Ice hockey has been described as a combination of "blood, sweat, and beauty." More than any other team sport, ice hockey is a game of motion: even when the action is whistled to a stop, the momentum

Right wing Patrick Kane raises the Stanley Cup in triumph after his team's championship win. **Bruce Bennett/Getty Images**

keeps flowing. The basic plays of the game are repeated endlessly, but the players are never able to skate in quite the same patterns, and the sequences of their moves keep changing. Fights are common, but even without the violence, ice hockey is a rugged game that demands superbly conditioned athletes. Serious injuries can result from the sheer speed of the action on the ice. Blood has hit the ice next to a player's skates many times, and players often sport gap-toothed grins due to teeth knocked out over the course of their careers. While at times controversial, to avid fans ice hockey's violence is part of the sport's tradition and shows passion and ferocity in players.

Canada has long been known to produce an extraordinary number of talented players, perhaps because the professional game was developed on Canadian ice. In addition, Canada in particular is known for having an exceptional number of passionate and enthusiastic fans. Ice hockey is so beloved in Canada that it is the country's national winter sport.

More than one million people play hockey in leagues around the world—and millions more watch them. From the development of the National Hockey League (NHL) to the stats of the greatest hockey players of all time, there's so much to learn about ice hockey. (For starters, for a game in which bare-knuckle brawls have become expected, one of the prestigious prizes is a trophy for the "most gentlemanly player.")

CHAPTER 1

ICE HOCKEY HISTORY AND THE NHL

Although casual games were played on makeshift ice skates in northern Europe during the Middle Ages, it wasn't until the 19th century that the modern sport of ice hockey truly began to emerge. Elements of ice hockey were influenced by the English game of field hockey and by lacrosse, a North American Indian game played with a stick, ball, and net. In the early 1800s, some North American Indians also played a game using field tools that were curved at the lower end, a derivation of the Irish and Scottish settlers' game of hurley, or hurling. This game evolved into an informal game on ice called shinny or shinty. French explorers who watched the Indians' improvised ball-and-stick games attached the French word for the similarly shaped shepherd's crook, *hoquet*—hockey.

This image from about 490 BCE shows a hockey-like sport played in Greece. **Gianni Dagi Orti/The Art Archive at Art Resource, NY**

During the 1700s and 1800s, moving about the ice on skates made with sharpened animal bones was a popular pastime, both in Europe and Canada. By the mid-1800s, a crude form of ice hockey was being played in Canada's frozen harbors by British troops stationed there. Rules and organization of the popular games were not far off.

ESTABLISHING THE GAME

Nineteenth–century Canadian lawyer, engineer, and athletic innovator James Creighton, a native of Halifax, Nova Scotia, is often credited with both the early rules of hockey and the organization of the first official, recorded game. As a boy, he and his friends had played pick-up games of shinny out on the ice. They would make the playing surface as long as needed for the number of people playing and choose the number of points it would take to win. Their games continued into their adult years as in 1875, the first indoor ice rink in Canada opened in Montreal, Quebec. Called the Victoria Skating Rink, it was used for figure skating competitions, at which Creighton sometimes served as a judge.

Three Canadian cities claim to be the locale of the first formal hockey game: Halifax; Montreal; and Kingston, Ontario. It is believed that some form of the game was being played in Kingston as early as 1830, twenty years before Creighton's birth. However, it was Creighton who organized the first recorded game. It was played at the Victoria Skating Rink on March 3, 1875. Members of the Montreal Football Club and students from McGill University formed

Some believe that James Creighton should be inducted into the Hockey Hall of Fame for his contributions to the modern game. Hockey Hall of Fame

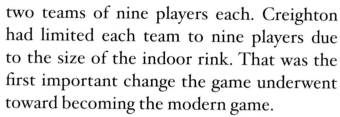

two teams of nine players each. Creighton had limited each team to nine players due to the size of the indoor rink. That was the first important change the game underwent toward becoming the modern game.

The second change was made with safety in mind. The Victoria Skating Rink had raised stands around it, but there was no glass protecting the spectators as there is in today's hockey rinks. The ball commonly used to play the game outdoors was thought to be too dangerous. (It was shot at high speeds, and spectators could have been seriously injured.) Therefore, a wooden disk 1 inch (2.5 centimeters) thick and 3 inches (7.6 centimeters) wide was used instead. It was soon known as a puck.

According to Canada's *Legion Magazine*, which includes stories about Canada's history, a local newspaper at the time, the *Gazette*, wrote that the game was "an interesting and well contested affair, the efforts of the players exciting much merriment as they wheeled and dodged each other." The *Gazette* went on to praise Creighton's winning goal as captain of one of the teams.

The teams played again on March 17, 1875. Only one game was played in 1876, but four were played in 1877. It was during this year that Creighton put together the first official rules for hockey, called the "Montreal" or "McGill" rules. They were published in the *Gazette* following an important game at the Victoria Skating Rink, including some rules still around today, such as the beginning face-off, an offside rule, and a rule against players' raising their sticks above shoulder height. Although the original game called for nine men on each side, the number of team players

Victoria Skating Rink, shown here, held the first Stanley Cup championship games in the 1893–94 season. **Hockey Hall of Fame**

RULES CANNOT STOP THE FIGHTS

The rules of hockey evolved over time—even while Creighton and others were developing them. His first set of hockey rules, called the "Halifax" rules, allowed the puck to be passed forward, but the official "Montreal" rules did not. Forward passing would not be allowed again for another fifty years, in 1929. Many changes, such as eliminating the rover in 1911, were intended to enhance gameplay, increase scoring, or otherwise make ice hockey more exciting.

Some rule changes have another goal—to decrease injury and violence. Since early in its history, hockey has been known as a somewhat brutal game. The *Daily British Whig* newspaper in Kingston reported of the first ice hockey game in 1875: "Shins and heads were battered, benches smashed and the lady spectators fled in confusion." Penalties against fighting and certain types of hitting have arisen over the years to help, as has the addition of safety equipment.

However, as American writer Adam Gopnik of the *New Yorker* reported in 2012, the Stanley Cup play-offs of that year included a Nashville player twice slamming the head of Detroit's Henrik Zetterberg against the glass and Raffi Torres of the Phoenix Coyotes not only beating on Chicago's Marian Hossa but also swearing at fans sitting behind the bench. Gopnik

Players from the Los Angeles Kings and the Phoenix Coyotes fight during the 2012 Stanley Cup play-offs. David E. Klutho/Sports Illustrated/Getty Images

attributes much of the "tradition" of violence to the "clan ethic" of hockey teams and fans. That is, that they are all willing to fight for their clan. Thus, rules, fines, and penalties can only do so much to stop players already out on the ice. Gopnik wrote that some fans say the hits keep ice hockey exciting, though he and others believe that it has gone too far: "Either the NHL is going to end the violence, or the violence is going to end the NHL."

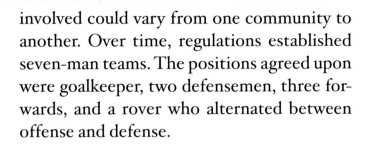

involved could vary from one community to another. Over time, regulations established seven-man teams. The positions agreed upon were goalkeeper, two defensemen, three forwards, and a rover who alternated between offense and defense.

GETTING ORGANIZED

The first hockey leagues were for amateurs. Two formed in the 1880s: one in Kingston and one in Montreal. For a time, it was seen as ungentlemanly to receive payment for playing a sport. That viewpoint did not last long. In 1904, the first professional hockey league was formed in Michigan, the International Pro Hockey League. Four years later, the Ontario Professional Hockey League was established. But it was the National Hockey Association's (NHA) formation in 1910 that really started the pro-hockey craze. The Pacific Coast Hockey Association (PCHA) formed in 1911 and contributed to the growing sport by building arenas that used artificial ice. Suddenly, places with warmer climates would be able to compete in ice hockey, too. A boom in construction of these rinks followed.

For several years, the NHA and PCHA competed for players, but the NHA proved to be the stronger league. In 1917, the NHA disbanded and reformed as the National Hockey League (NHL).

A Lasting League

Although the NHL was established in 1917, only six franchises remained a half century later—teams in Montreal; Toronto, Ontario;

The Montreal Maroons, shown playing here in 1932, were part of the NHL for 14 seasons. **Hockey Hall of Fame**

LORD STANLEY AND HIS CUP

The Stanley Cup is the oldest trophy that can be won by professional athletes in North America. Originally awarded to the best amateur hockey team in Canada, the cup bears the name of Frederick Arthur, Lord Stanley of Preston, who was a governor-general of Canada. He bought the cup for $50 in 1893 and it was awarded to the Montreal Amateur Athletic Association that year and in 1894. The trophy lent an air of legitimacy to ice hockey, paving the way for it to become seen as a more respected sport. In 1926, it became the official property of the NHL.

The Stanley Cup remains the coveted award given to the champions of the NHL. First, teams must win enough regular-season games to make the 16-team play-offs. Each of four play-off rounds involve best-of-seven

This photograph shows the Stanley Cup in 1902, when the Montreal Hockey Club won it. **Hulton Archive/Getty Images**

series, including the final Stanley Cup round. After winning the Stanley Cup, each member of the team—including managers, coaches, and others in the team office—get to spend a whole day with the cup! In 2003, after the New Jersey Devils won the NHL title, the team's goalie Martin Brodeur ate popcorn out of the Stanley Cup when he spent time with it. Dogs have also eaten out of it, as have players' children, making the Stanley Cup perhaps the most-used trophy in professional sports. Players have also taken the trophy with them into showers and pools. Today, a team of "cup cops" follows the Stanley Cup around as it tours each NHL title-winning city, just to make sure it's not lost forever or irreparably damaged!

Detroit, Michigan; Chicago, Illinois; New York, New York; and Boston, Massachusetts. In the period between 1926 and 1931, there had been a 10-team circuit. The advent of golden superstars such as Bobby Hull and Bobby Orr helped popularize the game in the United States. By 1974, the league had two nine-team conferences, each with two divisions.

The success of the NHL encouraged a rival league, the World Hockey Association (WHA), to begin operation in the 1972–73

season. The WHA lured about sixty players from the NHL. The WHA, which originally consisted of 12 teams, expanded to 14 in 1974. The league was realigned in 1976, again with 12 teams, but it cut back in 1977 and again in 1978. At the end of the 1978–79 season, four of the remaining six WHA teams were merged into the NHL. The other two WHA teams disbanded.

With the addition of the former WHA clubs, the NHL opened the 1979–80 season with a record 21 teams. The league experienced growth and reorganization during the 1990s, and by the early 21st century, it consisted of two 15-team conferences, each with three divisions. The Eastern Conference is split into Atlantic, Northeast, and Southeast divisions. The Western Conference consists of the Central, Northwest, and Pacific divisions. Each team plays an 82-game regular-season schedule that extends from the beginning of October into the first week of April. At the end of the season the top teams in each division engage in play-offs, and the overall winner receives the Stanley Cup.

CHAPTER 2
PLAYING THE GAME

I ce hockey is a particularly low-scoring, fast-moving game in which the team that hits the most pucks into its opponent's goal wins. The goals are located at each end of the hockey rink, an enclosed rectangular ice surface with rounded corners.

ON THE RINK

In the NHL, the rink is 200 feet (61 meters) long and 85 feet (26 meters) wide. These dimensions vary somewhat in other leagues. The rink is surrounded by wooden or fiberglass walls. Sideboards and end boards stand about 4 feet (1.2 meters) above the surface of the ice. Some of the roughest hockey action occurs when players are slammed into the boards. To protect the spectators, rinks also have shatterproof glass extending from the

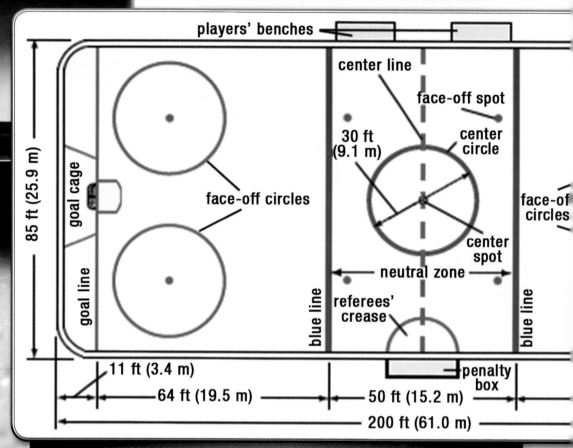

players' benches

center line

face-off spot

30 ft
(9.1 m)

center
circle

face-off circles

85 ft (25.9 m)

goal cage

goal line

face-off
circles

center
spot

neutral zone

blue line

referees'
crease

blue line

11 ft (3.4 m)

64 ft (19.5 m)

50 ft (15.2 m)

penalty
box

200 ft (61.0 m)

On every NHL rink, the lines and circles drawn on the ice are in specific spots for gameplay. Encyclopædia Britannica, Inc.

top of these boards. The glass also keeps the skaters, as well as the pucks, within the playing area.

For gameplay, the rink is divided into three zones. Drawn 60 feet (18.3 meters)

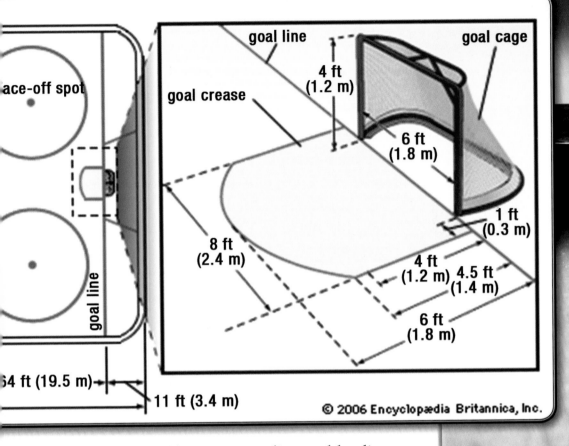

goal line

goal cage

ace-off spot

goal crease

4 ft (1.2 m)

6 ft (1.8 m)

1 ft (0.3 m)

8 ft (2.4 m)

4 ft (1.2 m)

4.5 ft (1.4 m)

6 ft (1.8 m)

goal line

54 ft (19.5 m)

11 ft (3.4 m)

© 2006 Encyclopædia Britannica, Inc.

from each goal line is a zone line, or blue line, extending across the width of the rink and up the sideboards. Each team's defensive zone is the area from this blue line back toward the goal the team is defending. Exactly between the two blue lines, at the middle of the rink, is the centerline, or red line. The ice surface between the blue lines is the neutral zone. A team's attacking, or offensive, zone is the area

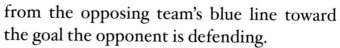

from the opposing team's blue line toward the goal the opponent is defending.

The ice surface also has markings for face-offs. A face-off is used to start or restart play whenever it has been stopped. It is initiated by one of the three officials (usually one referee and two linesmen), who drops the puck between two players, one from each team. In all, there are nine face-off spots, each one foot in diameter. Four of these are between the blue lines, and the other five are those enclosed by the face-off circles. One face-off circle, or area, 30 feet in diameter, is directly in center ice (neutral zone), and four other face-off circles are on either side of the goal cage in both defending zones.

Each goal is about 11 feet (3.4 meters) from the end boards of the rink. The goal is made up of a frame of two vertical posts 4 feet (1.2 meters) high and a horizontal bar 6 feet (1.8 meters) long across the top. Stretching from the posts to the ice level is a white net that encloses the sides and back and forms the cage into which the puck is shot. The goal is held in place on the ice with bright green flexible pegs. The only time a goal can be scored is when the puck completely crosses the goal line—a wide red border 2 inches (5 centimeters) thick that extends between the vertical goalposts.

Derick Brassard of the New York Rangers and Mike Richards of the Los Angeles Kings face off during the 2014 Stanley Cup Finals at Madison Square Garden, New York City. **Jim McIsaac/Getty Images**

GAMEPLAY

A hockey game is divided into three periods of 20 minutes each. In the NHL, intermissions between the periods are 17 minutes long. Most levels of the sport also provide for an overtime period if the score is tied. In the NHL, three periods resulting in a tie score are followed by a five-minute "sudden death" overtime period. That means, once a goal is scored, that team wins the game. If the game is still tied, the teams will then have a shootout in which one player at a time shoots on a goalie in net, undefended. Each team has three players shoot on goal with the hopes of scoring more than the other team.

Hockey is a speedy sport that demands a lot from its players. Unlike most other sports, ice hockey does not require that changes in personnel be made only when there is a stoppage in play. Substitutions often occur on the fly. Because action may proceed continuously for a period of several minutes, a player may skate over to his bench just off the ice and immediately be replaced by a teammate who plays the same position. The hazards of changing personnel on the fly are two-fold: it must be done at just the right time or the opponent will take advantage of the temporary shortage in manpower; and, if confusion occurs upon switching players, a team may end up with too many players on the ice and be given a penalty.

PLAYERS AND COACHES

Hockey teams usually carry 18 to 20 players and use most of them. Included are three forward lines and at least two pairs of defensemen, all of whom rotate on and off the ice. Those players on offense—the forwards— are commonly on the ice for only about ninety seconds. Defensemen may be out for a bit longer than that.

The forwards' primary goal is to move the puck toward the opposing team's goal and score. They do most of the penetration into the opponent's defensive zone and attempt most of their team's shots on the other team's goal. The center is often a clever stick handler with the major assignment of providing the puck to the two wings. Forward lines whose members are working well together usually pass the puck back and forth several times until they find an opening for a good shot. Although the forwards concentrate on offense, they are also depended on to guard the opposition. Sometimes they "check" an

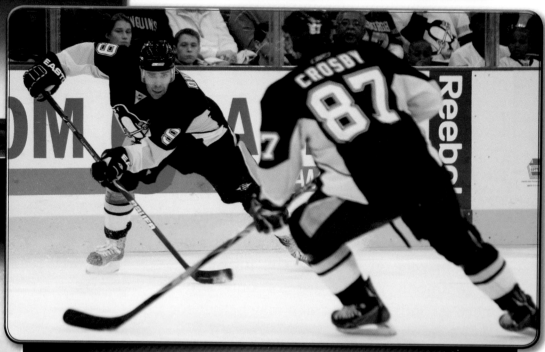

Players that are effective together often remain on the same line for a long time. **Jamie Sabau/Getty Images**

opposing player, or use body contact to take the opponent out of play.

The two defensemen are positioned behind the three forwards. Although defensemen frequently become involved directly in their team's offensive attempts, their primary duties are to limit the number of shots on goal and to break up scoring threats.

The last line of defense, the goalie, is entrusted with keeping the puck out of his team's net. With his stick, which is somewhat thicker than the other players' sticks, he steers the puck to a teammate or away from a foe. Directly in front of his net, the goalie stands in the crease, an area 4 feet (1.2 meters) by 8 feet (2.4 meters) drawn on the ice and into which the opposition is not supposed to enter unless the puck is also in the crease. If a player on the other team scores a goal while in this crease—provided that a member of the defending team hasn't pushed him into the area—the goal does not count. The goalie must always try to keep his eye on the puck, a task that is made even more arduous when players collect around his net. Protected by special safety equipment and extra padding, he has to handle all types of shots hurtled at his body. He may block these shots with any part of his equipment, or he may glove them and hold on, stopping play. The goalkeeper is the only player allowed to catch the puck in the glove.

Most teams will carry two goalkeepers but generally one plays for an entire game. His only rest comes when play is stopped, when the puck is at the other end of the rink, or during intermissions.

The last, and perhaps most influential, member of an ice hockey team is the

Good goalies, such as Corey Crawford of the Chicago Blackhawks, seen here catching a puck, have to be quite flexible to stop all kinds of shots.
Bill Smith/National Hockey League/Getty Images

head coach. The head coach is responsible for devising plays on the ice, encouraging players, and often dealing with confusing calls by officials. Besides the head coach, in many levels of ice hockey there are commonly several assistant coaches who work specially with the offense, defense, or goalies.

ICE HOCKEY EQUIPMENT

Ice hockey players of all levels use similar equipment. First, the puck is made of black vulcanized rubber, measuring 3 inches (7.6 centimeters) in diameter and 1 inch (2.5 centimeters) thick, with a weight of about 6 ounces (170 grams). The puck may move at speeds of more than 100 miles (161 kilometers) per hour! The primary tool hockey players use to move the puck is their wooden hockey stick. According to the NHL's official rules, sticks

(continued on the next page)

(continued from the previous page)

may not be more than 63 inches (160 centimeters) unless an exception is granted. Even then, a player's stick may not be more than 65 inches (165 centimeters). Regulations are in place for the length and curvature of the stick's blade, too.

Each player must have proper skates and padding, the latter of which must be worn under the uniform. Beginning in the 1979-80 season, all NHL players were required to wear helmets, which today are often accompanied

Goalies' equipment both keeps them from injury and helps them stop the puck. Here, Tuukka Rask of the Boston Bruins keeps his eye on an inbound shot. **Francois Laplante/FreestylePhoto/Getty Images**

by cage-like facemasks to protect a player's nose and mouth.

Ice hockey goalies wear significantly more equipment than do forwards and defensemen. In addition to wider and thicker pads, a goalie wears a mask to protect his entire face. He wears a glove that looks like a baseball mitt on one hand for catching the puck. On the hand used to hold his stick, he wears a glove with a wide back to block shots on net. The goalie's stick has a wider shaft and blade than those of the other players. When totally equipped, goalies may be wearing about 40 pounds (18 kilograms) of equipment.

PUCK DROP AND STOPPAGE OF PLAY

A game starts with a face-off at the center-ice face-off circle. The opposing centers try to gain possession of the puck or direct it to a teammate as the referee drops it. Either by passing the puck to a teammate in a better position or by carrying the puck himself, a player for the team in possession strives continually for a pattern that will produce the

best possible shot on the opponent's net. The better shots a team takes, the better chance it has of scoring.

There are limits on how a team may send the puck into an opponent's territory, and one of hockey's most important penalties—the offside penalty—is used to enforce these limits. A player may not pass the puck over two lines (either blue line and the red line) to a teammate, nor may a player precede the puck over the blue line into the opposition's territory. The position of the player's skates determines whether he is offside. Only if both of his skates have completely crossed the line in question (red or blue) is a player judged to be offside.

The administration of ice hockey penalties makes the game one of the few sports in which a team is deprived of a player after a transgression. The most prevalent penalty is the two-minute minor, which is assessed for such transgressions as holding, tripping, charging, elbowing, hooking, slashing, and interference. When a referee spots such an infraction, he will whistle the offender off the ice and send him to a penalty box. Penalties incurred by a goalie are served by a teammate. While a player is serving a penalty, his team may not replace him on the ice.

PENALTIES

Because hockey moves so quickly, it takes officials a good deal of practice to be able to spot penalties as players fly by them on the ice. Here is what they look for when calling some common penalties:

- **Cross checking:** a player makes a check while both his hands are still on his stick.
- **Hooking:** a player uses the blade of his stick to "hook" another player to stop him.
- **Roughing:** a player hits a member of the other team, but the referee doesn't see it as serious enough to be considered fighting.
- **Fighting:** players dropping their gloves and throwing punches.
- **Slashing:** a player uses his stick to hit, or slash, another player in order to stop or hurt him.
- **Tripping:** a stick, skate, or any part of a player's body causes another player to trip.

When a player is sitting in the penalty box and his team is playing shorthanded, the other team is on what's called a power play. They have a one-man advantage and often take the opportunity to try and score.

To date, the NHL record for penalty minutes served is 3,966—that is nearly 70 hours! Hannah Foslien/Getty Images

Until his time has expired, he may only leave the penalty box when his team, while short-handed, is scored against.

When a player is charged with a major penalty, he must serve the full time (five minutes), no matter how often his team is scored against. Major penalties are given for fighting with or injuring an opponent. If a player is guilty of insubordination to an official, he receives a 10-minute misconduct penalty. Misconduct suspensions may be given for abusive language, extended fighting, a second major penalty, or failure to proceed to the penalty box. When a player is benched for misconduct, his team doesn't have to play shorthanded. In extreme cases—for example, for joining a fight in progress—a player may receive an automatic game misconduct or match penalty, meaning that he is expelled from the game.

CHAPTER 3

ICE HOCKEY AROUND THE WORLD

As ice hockey organizations blossomed in Canada and then the United States, so, too, were international leagues growing around the world. Great Britain, Bohemia (part of the present-day Czech Republic), Switzerland, France, and Belgium founded the International Ice Hockey Federation (IIHF) in 1908. Soon, other nations also joined. More hockey organizations began to pop up in European countries, but none of these had a significant impact on the sport of ice hockey for most of the 20th century. Amateur athletes dominated international competition, including on the biggest international stage: the Olympics.

GOING FOR GOLD

Ice hockey made its first appearance as an Olympic sport during the 1920 Summer Games in Antwerp, Belgium. It became a permanent Winter Olympic sport beginning with the 1924 Games in Chamonix, France. By that time, ice hockey had already become a part of the fabric of Canadian life. Although professional players weren't yet allowed to play on Olympic teams, the Canadian men's ice hockey team dominated Olympic competition until 1956. That year, the Soviet Union went undefeated and won the gold medal. The Soviets won again in 1964—as well as the succeeding three Winter Olympics.

LET THEM PLAY!

One big change conclusively transformed international play in Olympic men's ice hockey. In 1995, the NHL, NHL Players' Association, and the IIHF agreed that professional players would be allowed to compete in the Olympics. Players would play for their home countries, not the countries in which they played professionally. The Winter Games of 1998 in Nagano, Japan, were full of

MIRACLE ON ICE

When the 1980 Winter Olympic Games began, the Soviet Union expected another glorious win by its men's ice hockey team. The Games were held in Lake Placid, New York, that year.

On February 22, 1980, the Soviet team played in a medal-round game against the United States. The U.S. team was full of young, unknown players who were amateurs and college players. The Soviet Union was heavily favored to win, heralded as the best team in the world at the time. Whoever lost the game would only have a chance for the silver or bronze medal, depending on the outcome of playing yet another game.

Team USA's 1980 victory was made into a movie called Miracle *in 2004.* Heinz Kluetmeier/ Sports Illustrated/Getty Images

The Soviet Union scored first—but U.S. player Buzz Schneider tied it up not quite five minutes later. Both teams scored again before the first period was over. By the second half of the third period, the game was tied at three. Then, Team USA got their only lead of the game when Mike Eruzione scored their fourth goal. It clinched their victory! Goalie Jim Craig blocked 36 of 39 shots in the U.S. goal.

Today, the upset is considered one of the greatest in history and is called the "miracle on ice." The U.S. team went on to defeat Finland for the gold medal that year. As of 2014, USA Hockey has two Olympic gold medals (the other win having come at the 1960 Games), as well as eight silver medals and one bronze.

pro hockey stars that had been playing in the NHL for years.

This choice raised the visibility of Olympic ice hockey considerably. All-Stars such as Brett Hull and Pat LaFontaine played for the United States. Canada's team was even more star-studded with Wayne Gretzky, Eric Lindros, and Martin Brodeur on the ice. These and other countries that were highly represented in the professional leagues had a great advantage, both with players and in advancement in the games that year.

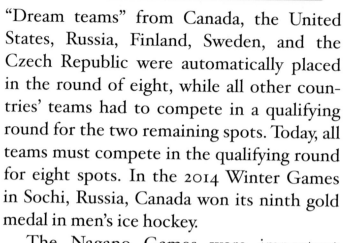

"Dream teams" from Canada, the United States, Russia, Finland, Sweden, and the Czech Republic were automatically placed in the round of eight, while all other countries' teams had to compete in a qualifying round for the two remaining spots. Today, all teams must compete in the qualifying round for eight spots. In the 2014 Winter Games in Sochi, Russia, Canada won its ninth gold medal in men's ice hockey.

The Nagano Games were important for another group of ice hockey players — women. Though the first recorded women's ice hockey game took place in Ontario, Canada, more than 100 years before, it wasn't until 1998 that women ice hockey players were included on the Olympic stage.

GOING PRO

The NHL continues to be the premier league in which to play hockey. No matter what country players represent in the Olympics, many begin their hockey careers as children hoping to one day play in the NHL. How can talented hockey players make their dream come true?

Most start out in development leagues. In Canada and the United States, where the

There are hockey leagues for kids as young as six years old! **Hero Images/Getty Images**

ice hockey development system is huge and multilevel, this process usually begins when a player is a teenager. Canadian junior hockey is a tiered system. The top tier is Major Junior Hockey, which is made up of the Quebec Major Junior Hockey League, the Ontario Hockey League, and the Western Hockey League. The players in these leagues are the best of the development league pool. The

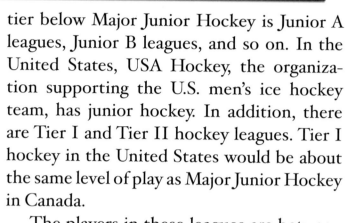

tier below Major Junior Hockey is Junior A leagues, Junior B leagues, and so on. In the United States, USA Hockey, the organization supporting the U.S. men's ice hockey team, has junior hockey. In addition, there are Tier I and Tier II hockey leagues. Tier I hockey in the United States would be about the same level of play as Major Junior Hockey in Canada.

The players in these leagues are between ages 16 and 20. They play in tournaments all over the United States and Canada, and it's at these tournaments that they'll be scouted for both college and professional teams. Unlike some other professional sports, ice hockey players don't need to play in college at all. Some play a few years in the hopes of being noticed by professional scouts, while others play in development leagues up until they're old enough to enter the draft. The choice of whether or not to go play ice hockey in college can be a tough one—but some players don't have that choice. Major Junior Hockey in Canada is considered the highest level of play for aspiring ice hockey players. However, the National Collegiate Athletic Association (NCAA) considers it professional ice hockey. Anyone who has played a sport professionally is ineligible to play in the NCAA.

The Edmonton Oil Kings, shown here in 2014, are the Major Junior Hockey team based in Edmonton, Alberta. **Bruce Bennett/Getty Images**

Many hockey players *do* go on to play some college hockey, about 30 percent according to the American sports network SB Nation (Sports Blog Nation). Because of draft rules, those who leave school at age 21 or over become free agents and do not need to take part in the draft. They can be signed by any NHL team, and many have gone on to achieve All-Star status, championships, and

Martin St. Louis, seen here in game four of the 2014 Stanley Cup Finals at Madison Square Garden, played some college hockey before playing for the New York Rangers. **Scott Levy/National Hockey League/Getty Images**

THE DRAFT

According to the NHL website, ice hockey players must be 19 years old or older to enter the draft, though 18-year-olds can enter under certain conditions with written notices to the league. Players not from North America can enter the draft at age 20.

The draft is the way NHL teams choose young, promising players to add to their team or American Hockey League (AHL) affiliate. The draft occurs once each year and has seven rounds — or seven picks per team, unless a team trades away its draft picks for players or future draft picks. The first team to pick is chosen by a lottery entered by the 14 teams that didn't make the play-offs. Then, the remaining 13 teams draft from lowest to highest point total, calculated by wins (2), losses (0), and ties (1 if lost in overtime) from the previous regular season. Teams that did make the play-offs make their picks next. The Stanley Cup champions have the last draft pick.

play in the Olympics. Martin St. Louis was first signed in 1997 after playing ice hockey for the University of Vermont. To date, he's played in six NHL All-Star Games, won the

Stanley Cup once, and earned an Olympic gold medal with Team Canada.

The AHL

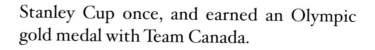

The American Hockey League (AHL) is the "top development league for the National Hockey League," according to the AHL website. Sometimes the AHL is simply called minor league hockey. Each team in the AHL is affiliated with an NHL team, serving as that team's "farm team." A few farm teams exist outside of the AHL, and the Anaheim Ducks don't have an AHL affiliate.

The AHL is a place for young players to hone their skills on the ice and increase their professional playing experience. Most of the players in the AHL have been chosen by the NHL draft and have contracts with an NHL team. As of the end of the 2014 season, 87 percent of the current players in the NHL played in the AHL, according to the AHL website. The other 13 percent include drafted players who are deemed skilled enough to play in the NHL without a stint in the AHL or who played in junior leagues in other places, such as Europe.

Coaches and managers of the NHL affiliate closely watch the players on their farm teams. If a trade or injury opens up a spot on the NHL bench during the season, an AHL player needs to be ready to play if he is "called up." This makes an AHL team's season somewhat unpredictable.

PRO WOMEN

The steps to becoming a professional ice hockey player are still difficult for

The Toronto Furies, champions of the 2014 Canadian Women's Hockey League, win a trophy called the Clarkson Cup. **Andrew Francis Wallace/Toronto Star/Getty Images**

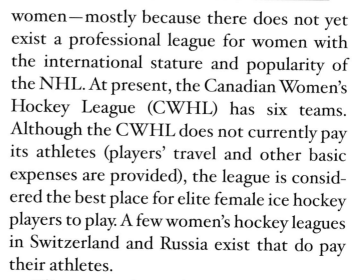

women—mostly because there does not yet exist a professional league for women with the international stature and popularity of the NHL. At present, the Canadian Women's Hockey League (CWHL) has six teams. Although the CWHL does not currently pay its athletes (players' travel and other basic expenses are provided), the league is considered the best place for elite female ice hockey players to play. A few women's hockey leagues in Switzerland and Russia exist that do pay their athletes.

Elite women's ice hockey players often play on World Championship or Olympic teams, but those aren't year-round jobs. As more women players leave successful college careers, many of them will continue to look for places to play. The CWHL's website states its aim as "raising the profile of women's hockey while providing a place where the best female hockey players in the world can train and compete."

CHAPTER 4

ICE HOCKEY GREATS

MARTIN BRODEUR

Martin Brodeur became the goal-tender to win the most games ever in NHL history in March 2009. Moreover, he's one of the only goalies to score a goal in an NHL play-off game!

Brodeur was born on May 6, 1972, in Montreal, Quebec, Canada. His father had been a player for the Canadian Olympic ice hockey team in 1956. Brodeur was a first-round choice of the 1990 NHL draft and signed with the New Jersey Devils. His breakout season occurred in 1993–94, when he won the Calder Memorial Trophy as the league's top rookie.

During the 1994–95 season, Brodeur helped his team win the Stanley Cup champi-onship. He then became a fixture in goal for

A fixture on Canada's Olympic hockey team, Martin Brodeur is one of the greatest goalies ever. Luis Acosta/AFP/Getty Images

the Devils and in the NHL's All-Star Game. Between the 1997–98 and 2007–08 seasons, he played in at least 70 regular-season games each year. An excellent stickhandler, Brodeur in 1997 became the second goaltender in NHL history to score a goal in a play-off game. He led the Devils to Stanley Cup victories in 2000 and 2003.

Brodeur was a member of Team Canada in the Olympic Games four times. At the Salt Lake City 2002 Games, he played a significant role in the team's gold medal win. Two years after winning Olympic gold, Brodeur helped Team Canada win the World Cup championships. He won a second Olympic gold medal at the Vancouver 2010 Games.

Throughout his career Brodeur earned numerous honors and broke many records. He won the Vezina Trophy for the league's most outstanding goaltender four times between 2002 and 2008. He holds the record for 40-win seasons (8) and most consecutive 30-win seasons (12). In December 2009, he played in his 1,030th regular-season game, an all-time NHL record for a goaltender. Later that month, Brodeur set another record when he registered his 104th shutout, surpassing the mark set by goalie Terry Sawchuk.

Wayne Gretzky

Wayne Gretzky is the only hockey player to have his uniform number, 99, retired league-wide in the NHL. His finesse and speed revolutionized how the sport of ice hockey is played today.

Born on January 26, 1961, in Brantford, Ontario, Canada, Gretzky began skating at age two and a half. By age six he was playing as an All-Star in novice hockey with boys 10 and 11 years old. In the 1977 Junior World Cup competition, he was the youngest player and the leading scorer.

Gretzky turned professional for the 1978–79 season, playing for the Indianapolis Racers in the WHA. His contract soon was sold to the Edmonton Oilers, who joined the NHL at the beginning of the 1979–80 season. As center and team captain, Gretzky led the Oilers to four Stanley Cup victories between the 1983–84 season and the 1987–88 season. He was then traded to the Los Angeles Kings.

Gretzky had many notable moments in the NHL. During the 1980–81 season, he became the first player in NHL history to average more than two points a game. In the 1981–82 season, he set NHL regular-season scoring records for goals (92), assists (120),

Wayne Gretzky at a press conference after having scored his 802nd goal, March 24, 1994. **B Bennett/Hulton Archive/Getty Images**

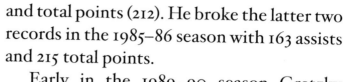

and total points (212). He broke the latter two records in the 1985–86 season with 163 assists and 215 total points.

Early in the 1989–90 season Gretzky broke Gordie Howe's NHL all-time scoring record of 1,850 points (the total number of goals and assists), and late in the 1993–94 season he broke Howe's record for career goals (801). In 1996, Gretzky was traded by the Los Angeles Kings to the St. Louis Blues. Later that year he signed with the New York Rangers. With his 1,851st assist, scored in a 1997 game against the Anaheim Mighty Ducks, Gretzky broke yet another record, scoring more assists than any player had scored points in an NHL career.

Gretzky retired from professional play after the 1998–99 season and was inducted into the Hockey Hall of Fame in 1999. His career totals include 2,857 points and 894 goals.

GORDIE HOWE

Gordie Howe entertained fans with his skill and competitive fire for three decades. He became known for the "Gordie Howe hat-trick," which was comprised of a goal, an assist, and a fight in a single game. His career

Gordie Howe earned a fitting nickname during his time on the ice: "Mr. Hockey." Walter Iooss Jr./Sports Illustrated/Getty Images

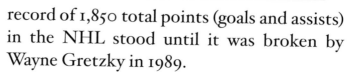

record of 1,850 total points (goals and assists) in the NHL stood until it was broken by Wayne Gretzky in 1989.

Howe was born on March 31, 1928, in Floral, Saskatchewan, Canada. He played hockey from the age of five. He was signed to a contract for Omaha in 1945 and played a season there before joining the Detroit Red Wings in 1946. He won the Hart Trophy for the most valuable player of the season several times and was named Canada's Athlete of the Year in 1963. Howe left the Red Wings in 1971 to play for and become the vice president (president from 1973) of the Houston Aeros in the WHA. He played for the Aeros through 1977, five years after he was inducted into the Hockey Hall of Fame. For part of the time, two of his sons were on the team, too!

During his 33-season career, Howe had 1,071 goals (801 in the NHL) and 1,518 assists (1,049 in the NHL) and played in 2,421 games.

BOBBY HULL

Bobby Hull had great skating speed and a bullet-like shot that earned him the nickname "Golden Jet." He was inducted into the Hockey Hall of Fame in 1983. His son

Bobby Hull played professional hockey for 23 years. James Drake/
Sports Illustrated/Getty Images

Brett Hull also was an outstanding player in the NHL and was himself inducted into the Hockey Hall of Fame in 2009.

Bobby Hull was born on January 3, 1939, in Point Anne, Ontario, Canada. At age 12, Hull was playing organized hockey on a team with his father. He later dropped out of school to join the Chicago Blackhawks in 1957, at first playing center but later forward. In the 1959–60 season, Hull led the NHL in scoring with 39 goals, and two seasons later he scored 50 goals, matching a record set by Maurice Richard. In 1965–66, Hull established a new record with 54 goals, 43 assists, and 97 points. In 1961, he helped the Blackhawks win the Stanley Cup.

In 1972, Hull joined the Winnipeg Jets of the WHA. He played with the Jets from 1972 to 1979 (serving as player-coach from 1972 to 1974), and in the 1974–75 season he scored seventy-seven goals. He returned to the NHL when the Jets were absorbed into the league in 1979. He played 18 games with the Jets before being traded to the Hartford Whalers, and he retired after the 1979–80 season.

His final totals included 610 NHL goals, 560 assists, and 1,170 points; and in the WHA, 303 goals, 335 assists, and 638 points.

MARIO LEMIEUX

Mario Lemieux was born on October 5, 1965, in Montreal, Quebec, Canada. His star rose early. As a teenager in the Quebec Major Junior Hockey League, Lemieux set a league record by scoring 282 points in 70 games during the 1983–84 season. The Pittsburgh Penguins chose him with the first overall selection in the 1984 NHL draft.

Lemieux had an outstanding rookie season: he scored 100 points, was named to the All-Star team, and was awarded the Calder Memorial Trophy as the NHL's rookie of the year. He scored more than 100 points in each of his first six years in Pittsburgh and was named NHL Most Valuable Player (MVP) for the 1987–88 season, even though the Penguins only qualified for the play-offs once during that period. Injury and illness kept Lemieux off the ice for much of the early 1990s. He returned at full strength in 1995–96, leading the league in all scoring categories on his way to a third career MVP award. He retired in 1997 at age 31. He was inducted into the Hockey Hall of Fame later that year. In 1999, Lemieux led a group of investors that jointly purchased the Penguins. He came out of retirement and returned to the Penguins

Mario Lemieux bounced back in a big way after major health issues kept him off the ice. He is seen here in 1996, hand atop the Hart Memorial Trophy, an annual award given to the league's MVP.
B Bennett/Getty Images

during the 2000–01 season, becoming the first player-owner in NHL history.

In 2002, Lemieux captained the Canadian Olympic hockey team to a gold medal at the Salt Lake City (Utah) Games. Lemieux retired for a second and final time mid-way through the 2005–06 season. Lemieux placed ninth on the NHL's all-time goals scored list, tenth all-time in assists, and seventh all-time in total points at the time of his second retirement. The Penguins won their third Stanley Cup in 2008–09, and Lemieux became the first person to win the cup as both a player and an owner.

BOBBY ORR

Bobby Orr was born on March 20, 1948, in Parry Sound, Ontario, Canada. He was the first defenseman to lead the NHL in scoring.

Orr came to the attention of the Boston Bruins when he was 12, and he was signed to a junior amateur contract. He joined the Bruins in 1966, when he had reached the legally required age of 18, and he played with them for 10 seasons. Orr helped the Bruins to the play-offs for eight consecutive seasons and to two Stanley Cups. Orr was a highly

Bobby Orr scored the game- and championship-winning goal for the Bruins in 1970. **B Bennett/Getty Images**

decorated player and received more than 16 major awards in his career, including the Norris Trophy as most valuable defenseman (1967–75). During the 1968–69 season, he scored 21 goals and made 43 assists (64 points) for a season record for a defenseman. In his career he set seasonal defenseman records for goals (46), assists (102), and points (139).

Orr retired in 1979, the same year of his induction into the Hockey Hall of Fame. After his retirement as a player, Orr received the Lester Patrick Trophy for outstanding contributions to hockey in the United States.

Jacques Plante

Jacques Plante was an innovative French-Canadian hockey player who became one of the most successful goaltenders in NHL history. He was an integral member of the powerful Montreal Canadiens team that won a record five successive Stanley Cups (1956–60). Following his pioneering example, nearly all subsequent goaltenders wore protective facemasks. Hit by a slap shot in a 1959 game, Plante received 21 facial stitches. Then, as Montreal's only goalie, he returned to the ice wearing a facemask.

The Montreal Canadiens retired Jacques Plante's #1 jersey in 1995.
Denis Brodeur/National Hockey League/Getty Images

Plante was born on January 17, 1929, in Shawinigan Falls, Quebec, Canada. While an amateur, Plante developed his unorthodox goaltending style, roaming behind his net to clear pucks from opposing players. His first NHL game, during the 1952 play-offs, was a shutout, and he went on to win 82 shutouts in 837 regular-season games and 15 shutouts in 112 play-off games.

As a Canadien, Plante won six Vezina Trophies for the league's best goalie, including five in a row. After the 1962–63 season, he played for the New York Rangers, the St. Louis Blues (where he shared his seventh Vezina Trophy), the Toronto Maple Leafs, and the Boston Bruins. Plante also played one season (1974–75), his last in the majors, for the Edmonton Oilers of the WHA, where he recorded 15 wins, including one shutout. Plante died on February 26, 1986, in Geneva, Switzerland.

CONCLUSION

Though the history of hockey is full of players with impressive scoring records and years-long domination in the play-offs, it is first and foremost a team sport. Greats such as Gretzky and Orr would never have risen to such heights without skilled teammates to pass to or get passes from. Goalies such as Brodeur must back up high scorers because wins are hard to come by without someone protecting the goal well.

The speed, agility, and timing needed to be a successful ice hockey player take years to acquire, and with dedication and practice many have found their home out on the ice. The sport continues to grow. In 2014, the Champions Hockey League began, pitting Europe's top teams against one another. Whether it will ever be able to compete with the NHL is unknown—though it is a fun question for fans to ponder. What players have the potential to be hockey greats is unknown, too, but wherever such players emerge, fans around the world will continue to enjoy watching these future stars of the ice develop. One exciting moment could change the outcome of a game—or career—quickly. Hockey fanatics *do* know one thing: the hits will keep on coming!

affiliate A person or organization with which one has a connection.

amateur Having to do with a job done without pay. Also, someone who does something without pay.

controversial Relating to a strong difference of opinion on a matter.

coveted Strongly desired.

crook A shepherd's staff with one end curved into a hook.

elite Describing the group having the highest quality.

evolved Grew and changed over time.

franchise A professional sports team that is a member of an organized league.

free agent A player whose contract has ended or who does not have a contract, allowing him to sign a contract with a new team.

ineligible Not qualified to be chosen or used.

infraction A break in a sport's rules.

insubordination Having to do with not obeying authority.

intermission A break in gameplay.

legitimacy Having to do with being seen as purposeful and established.

neutral Not belonging to or favoring either side in a contest, game, or any kind of competition.

offside Rule requiring that an offensive player not pass the two defenders closest to the goal until the puck is played to him. The rule prevents players from lurking about the goal all game, but it can be difficult to judge.

overtime The extra time of play beyond a game's set limit.

penetration The act of moving into an opponent's area.

pick-up game A spontaneous, unofficiated game often played with friends or random people.

play-off Games played after the regular season to decide upon a champion.

premier First in position, rank, or importance.

replay To rerun part of a recording, especially to be able to more closely watch a fast-moving segment of a game.

retire To leave a job.

scout Someone who searches for people with great skills in a sport.

spectator Someone watching a sporting event.

sudden death An overtime competition played in order to break a tie. The game ends the moment one side scores.

tier Level or rank.

unorthodox Not traditional.

vulcanized Rubber or a similar plastic material chemically treated in order to give it useful properties such as flexibility or strength.

wing Player on either side of a center position on the forward (offensive) line.

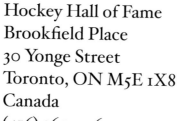

Hockey Hall of Fame
Brookfield Place
30 Yonge Street
Toronto, ON M5E 1X8
Canada
(416) 360-7765
E-mail: info@hhof.com
Website: http://www.hhof.com
The Hockey Hall of Fame celebrates great
players and moments in ice hockey's history. With new inductions every year,
it is a great place to learn more about
the game and those who have played it
exceptionally well.

National Hockey League Players'
Association (NHLPA)
20 Bay Street, Suite 1700
Toronto, ON M5J 2N8
Canada
(416) 313-2300
Website: http://www.nhlpa.com
The NHLPA represents the players
of the NHL in all contract and labor
matters. The organization also
takes part in numerous charitable
initiatives, including the Goals &
Dreams Fund.

SABAH
2607 Niagara Street
Buffalo, NY 14207
(716) 362-9600
E-mail: Sabah@sabahinc.org
Website: http://www.sabahinc.org
SABAH—or Skating Athletes Bold at
    Heart—partners with NHL players and
    skaters as well as community volunteers
    to bring ice skating to those with physi-
    cal or developmental handicaps.

USA Hockey Foundation
Walter L. Bush Jr. Center
1775 Bob Johnson Drive
Colorado Springs, CO 80906-4090
Website: http://www
    .usahockeyfoundation.com
(719) 538-1107
The USA Hockey Foundation funds the
    USA Hockey program, as well as works to
    bring ice hockey to communities around
    the United States.

Wayne Gretzky Foundation
245 King George Road, Suite 302
Brantford, ON N3R 7N7
Canada

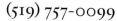

(519) 757-0099
Website: http://www.gretzky.com/foundation
Hockey great Wayne Gretzky founded
   this organization in 2002. It brings ice
   hockey to those who are less fortunate
   and helps teach other life and social
   skills as well.

WEBSITES

Because of the changing nature of Internet
links, Rosen Publishing has developed an
online list of websites related to the subject
of this book. This site is updated regularly.
Please use this link to access this list:

http://www.rosenlinks.com/SPOR/Hock

Carty, Michelle. *Give It Your All: The Olympic Sport of Ice Hockey.* Cypress, CA: Creative Teaching Press, 2002.

Doeden, Matt. *Wayne Gretsky.* Minneapolis, MN: Twenty-First Century Books, 2008.

Hurley, Michael. *Ice Hockey.* Mankato, MN: Capstone Raintree, 2013.

Johnson, Tami. *Girls' Ice Hockey: Dominating the Rink.* Mankato, MN: Capstone Press, 2008.

McFee, Shane. *Let's Play Ice Hockey.* New York, NY: Rosen Publishing, 2008.

National Hockey League. "2012-2013 Official NHL Rulebook." Retrieved May 30, 2014 (http://www.nhl.com/ice/page .htm?id=27011).

Sandler, Michael. *Hockey: Miracle on Ice.* New York, NY: Bearport, 2006.

Sharp, Anne Wallace. *Ice Hockey.* San Diego, CA: Lucent Books, 2011.

Wiseman, Blaine. *Stanley Cup.* New York, NY: Weigl Publishers, 2011.